EPICARICACY

From Shadow Joy to Beautiful Thinking

SHYAMANKAR SINGHARI

Epicaricacy: From Shadow Joy to Beautiful Thinking

ISBN: 978-81-992623-5-5

Publisher: WKRISHIND

wkrishind.in

Dedication

To everyone who has ever felt the shadow of envy or the flicker of epicaricacy—may you discover that real joy lies not in another's stumble, but in the shared beauty of rising together.

Acknowledgments

This book would not have been possible without the encouragement and inspiration of those who have walked alongside me on my own journey.

To my friends and mentors, who reminded me that success multiplies when shared—thank you for your wisdom and patience.

To the countless readers, students, and clients who opened up about their struggles with comparison and envy—you gave this book its heartbeat.

And to my family, who taught me what eunoia truly looks like in everyday life—this book is as much yours as it is mine.

Author's Note

When I first came across the word *epicaricacy*, I was struck by how familiar it felt. A rare word, yes—but the experience it names is anything but rare. We all know that flicker of shadow joy. And we all know the hollowness that follows.

This book began as an exploration of that word but became something much larger: a map of transformation. Alongside Adrian's fictional journey, you'll find pieces of my own story woven in—times when I struggled with envy, with comparison, with the temptation to root against others instead of celebrating them.

Writing this book was not just an act of teaching, but of healing. I hope, as you read, that you don't just see Adrian in these pages—you see yourself. And more importantly, that you see the possibility of something brighter.

If there is one message I hope you carry away, it is this: joy is never scarce. It multiplies when shared. And when we shift from epicaricacy to eunoia, we discover not only better relationships, but a better version of ourselves.

Thank you for letting me share this journey with you.

— Shyamankar Singhari

Table of Contents

Chapter 1

A Smile in the Dark

Adrian Vale leaned back in his chair, arms crossed, as the conference room projector flickered. Marcus—the golden boy of the marketing department—was sweating bullets at the podium. His slide deck froze, his voice cracked, and his carefully rehearsed pitch dissolved into nervous stammering.

Adrian's lips twitched. He fought it at first, but the corners of his mouth betrayed him. A smile. A quiet, delicious satisfaction crept in as he watched Marcus struggle.

It wasn't that Adrian hated Marcus. In fact, they had been colleagues for years, exchanging polite hellos and Friday afternoon jokes. But Marcus had always been one step ahead—praised in meetings, first in line for promotions, the one people looked toward when big projects landed.

Now here he was, faltering. Failing.

And it felt good.

Adrian's chest filled with a perverse warmth. It was the same sensation he felt when a rival tripped in a marathon, when a neighbor's expensive car sputtered and broke down, when a friend's social media brag was followed by an embarrassing apology.

It wasn't kindness. It wasn't empathy. It was something darker—pleasure drawn not from victory, but from another's downfall.

The room was quiet, except for Marcus's faltering voice. A few colleagues coughed awkwardly. Someone muttered encouragement. But Adrian remained still, hiding his satisfaction behind a neutral expression. He knew he shouldn't feel this way. He knew it was petty, small. Yet the thrill lingered like a secret he didn't want to give up.

Later, as Marcus stumbled out of the room, Adrian caught his own reflection in the polished glass of the conference door. His smile had faded, leaving only a faint shadow of it behind.

Why did it feel so good to see someone else fail? And why did that same pleasure feel… empty, the moment it ended?

Reflection: The Shadow of Epicaricacy

What Adrian felt has a name: **epicaricacy**—the secret joy in another's misfortune.

It's more common than most admit. Psychologists suggest it often arises from **insecurity, competition, or comparison**. When someone else stumbles, we temporarily feel taller, safer, even vindicated.

But the satisfaction is fragile. Like Adrian, many discover it fades quickly, leaving hollowness behind.

Ask Yourself:

- Have you ever caught yourself smiling at someone else's failure?
- Did it truly satisfy you—or did the feeling vanish, replaced by something else (guilt, emptiness, or even shame)?
- What does that moment reveal about what you really wanted?

Exercise – Awareness Without Judgment

For the next week, simply notice when you feel flashes of epicaricacy.

- Write them down in a journal.
- Don't scold yourself. Just observe.

- Ask: What insecurity in me was fed by this?

Awareness is the first step. Only when we can name the shadow can we begin to move toward light.

Chapter 2

A Hollow Kind of Victory

The office buzzed the next morning with whispers about Marcus's disastrous presentation. By the coffee machine, two colleagues exchanged knowing smirks. In the break room, someone chuckled under their breath, "Guess the golden boy's shine finally wore off."

Adrian sipped his coffee, listening but saying nothing. Inside, though, he felt a surge of quiet triumph. For once, it wasn't him fumbling under pressure. For once, Marcus was the one under the microscope.

By lunch, Adrian had been summoned to the manager's office. "Marcus will be stepping back from the client account," his boss explained. "I'd like you to take the lead."

Adrian nodded with a mask of humility, but the thrill was unmistakable. The opportunity he had been waiting for was here—delivered not because he had outperformed, but because someone else had failed.

That night, Adrian celebrated alone with a glass of whiskey. He told himself he had earned it. He had been overlooked too many times. Now it was his turn.

Yet as he scrolled through the project files, preparing to take over, a strange emptiness crept in.

The victory didn't feel like his. It felt borrowed.

Worse, he caught himself hoping Marcus wouldn't recover too quickly, that his colleague might stumble again so Adrian could rise further. The thought unsettled him, but he didn't push it away.

At the bottom of his glass, Adrian wondered: if his success depended on others' failures, what would that make of him in the long run?

Reflection: The Cost of Comparison-Driven Success

Adrian's rise was real—but it was built on someone else's stumble. This is the trap of *epicaricacy*: success feels sweeter when it comes at another's expense, but the satisfaction rarely lasts.

Why? Because it isn't rooted in **growth** or **authentic achievement**—it's rooted in comparison. And comparison always moves the goalposts. Someone will always be ahead, or behind, and the cycle of envy and hollow victories continues.

Ask Yourself:

- Have you ever celebrated a "win" that came more from someone else losing than from your own effort?
- Did the satisfaction last—or did it fade quickly?
- How does this mindset limit your own growth?

Exercise – The Source of Your Wins

1. Write down 3 recent successes you've had.
2. For each, ask: Did I earn this through my effort, or because someone else faltered?
3. If it came from someone else's loss, ask yourself: How can I build on this opportunity in a way that reflects my own growth?

The goal isn't to reject opportunities—it's to shift focus from what others lose to what you can truly gain.

Chapter 3

The Mirror Breaks

Clara's voice cracked over the phone.

"I lost the contract, Adrian. Months of work… gone. They went with another agency."

Adrian sat at his desk, pen frozen above his notepad. He heard the strain in her words, the way she tried to mask devastation with forced calm. Clara had always been steady—his anchor through college nights, first jobs, heartbreaks. She was the one person who had never seemed to falter.

And yet, for the briefest flicker of a second, something inside him stirred. That familiar warmth. The same twisted spark he felt when Marcus's slides froze.

She had failed.

And before he could stop it, the thought carried a cruel comfort: maybe she wasn't untouchable after all.

But then—like glass shattering—the realization struck him. This wasn't Marcus. This wasn't a rival or a coworker he envied. This was Clara. His friend. The one who had believed in him when no one else did.

The flicker of satisfaction died instantly, leaving behind only a sick hollowness. His chest tightened as shame rushed in.

"Clara… I'm so sorry," he managed, forcing the words past the lump in his throat.

She sighed. "Yeah. Just feels like I'm back at square one."

Adrian wanted to comfort her, but all he could hear was his own silence—the silence of the moment when he had almost enjoyed her pain. He saw himself clearly then, as though looking in a mirror he had been avoiding for years.

The reflection was not flattering.

He ended the call with promises of support, but long after, the echo of his own reaction haunted him. For the first time, Adrian wondered if the joy he took in others' failures was less a harmless quirk and more a sickness.

And if it could taint his friendship with Clara… what else could it destroy?

Reflection: When Shadow Joy Touches What We Love

This chapter highlights the breaking point of *epicaricacy*: when it crosses into the lives of people we care about. The illusion shatters. What once felt like harmless satisfaction reveals itself as a destructive force, even to our closest bonds.

Ask Yourself:

- Have you ever felt envy or secret relief at the misfortune of someone you love?
- How did that moment affect your relationship —or your view of yourself?
- What does this reveal about the deeper insecurities driving those feelings?

Exercise – The Mirror Check

1. Write down the names of three people you truly care about.
2. Ask yourself honestly: If they failed at something important, how would I feel? Relief? Satisfaction? Or genuine empathy?

3. If any trace of shadow joy appears, don't judge yourself. Instead, ask: *What fear or insecurity in me is being soothed by their stumble?*

When we face these uncomfortable truths, we give ourselves the power to change them. The mirror may be harsh, but it also shows us where to begin.

Chapter 4

The Mentor's Warning

The café was nearly empty, save for the hum of the espresso machine and the occasional clink of ceramic cups. Adrian sat across from Mr. Harrow, his former professor turned mentor, a man whose calm presence seemed to sharpen rather than soften truths.

"You look distracted," Harrow said, stirring his tea.

Adrian shifted uncomfortably. He had intended to ask for advice on managing his new account, but the weight of Clara's phone call lingered. And deeper still, the shame of his reaction gnawed at him.

"I've been… noticing things about myself," Adrian admitted. "Things I don't like."

Harrow leaned forward. "Go on."

Adrian hesitated, then spoke carefully. "I realized I feel… satisfaction when others fail. At work, with friends—even Clara. For a moment, I was glad she stumbled. It was like… I wanted it."

The confession hung between them, heavy and raw.

Harrow's eyes didn't flinch. Instead, he nodded slowly. "You've just described a word most people don't know. *Epicaricacy.* Joy at another's misfortune."

Adrian blinked. Hearing it named made it feel both alien and painfully real.

"Is it normal?" he asked.

Harrow set down his spoon. "It's human. But normal doesn't mean harmless. Think of it this way—if your victories depend on others falling, what foundation are you standing on? Sand. It won't last."

Adrian looked down at his hands, silent.

Harrow continued, his voice steady but firm. "You can feed on scraps of failure your whole life. But it will never nourish you. At best, it makes you dependent. At worst, it rots you from the inside."

The words struck deep. Adrian felt exposed, as though Harrow had read the thoughts he hadn't dared to speak aloud.

"So what do I do?" Adrian finally asked.

Harrow smiled faintly. "The opposite. Stop looking down for satisfaction and start looking up. Learn to celebrate growth—not collapse. When you can find joy in others rising, you'll finally learn how to rise yourself."

For the first time in days, Adrian felt both fear and hope. Fear of what he might become if he stayed the same. Hope that there might be another way forward.

Reflection: The Danger of Living on Scraps

Mr. Harrow's warning is clear: living through others' failures keeps us small. Epicaricacy is seductive because it gives us momentary relief from our own insecurities. But in the long run, it leaves us weaker, dependent, and unsatisfied.

Ask Yourself:

- Do I rely on others' mistakes to feel better about myself?
- What happens to my sense of worth when others succeed?
- Am I building a foundation on sand—or on my own growth?

Exercise – The "Sand or Stone" Test

1. Think of your last three personal wins.

2. For each, ask: Was this built on my own effort (stone) or on someone else's failure (sand)?
3. Circle the "sand" wins and write down one concrete action to turn them into "stone" wins by adding your own growth, skill, or effort.

Real success isn't borrowed—it's built.

Chapter 5

The Turning Point

The office was unusually tense. A junior colleague, Maya, was about to give her first presentation to the client team. Adrian watched her shuffle her notes with trembling fingers. He recognized the fear instantly—it was the same fear Marcus had faced weeks earlier, the same fear that had once been his own.

Old habits stirred. He felt the familiar anticipation of watching someone stumble. But Harrow's words echoed in his mind: *"You can feed on scraps of failure your whole life. But it will never nourish you."*

Adrian sat back, wrestling with himself. He could let the scene unfold, collect another secret thrill… or he could try something different.

He leaned forward.

"Maya," he whispered, just before she began, "you've got this. Just speak like you did in rehearsal—it was solid."

She glanced at him, startled, then nodded.

The presentation began. At first, her voice wavered, but Adrian noticed her steadying, gaining confidence.

When she made a strong point, he gave a subtle nod of encouragement. By the end, she had the room's attention—and applause.

Adrian felt… strange. There was no surge of dark pleasure, no secret smile at another's stumble. Instead, there was a quiet pride, not in himself, but in her. It wasn't the wild rush of epicaricacy. It was softer, steadier—like light filling a dim room.

Later, Maya approached him. "Thanks for that. I was terrified, but knowing you were rooting for me—it helped."

Adrian smiled back, genuinely this time. He realized he had discovered a different kind of joy. Not the brittle satisfaction of someone falling, but the enduring warmth of helping someone rise.

It wasn't easy. It wasn't natural yet. But it was a start.

Reflection: Small Shifts, Big Momentum

Adrian's choice to encourage rather than anticipate failure marked his first step out of the cycle of epicaricacy. Change doesn't begin with grand gestures —it begins with small, intentional choices.

The difference between shadow-joy and light-joy is simple: one feeds off weakness, the other builds strength.

Ask Yourself:

- When was the last time I actively encouraged someone, rather than silently waiting for them to fail?
- How did it feel compared to shadow-joy?
- What small encouragement could I offer someone today?

Exercise – The One Encouragement Rule

For the next week:

1. Each day, choose one person in your circle—colleague, friend, or family member.
2. Offer them genuine encouragement (a kind word, acknowledgment, or support).
3. At night, write down how it made you feel.

Notice the difference between fleeting satisfaction from others' missteps and the lasting fulfillment of helping someone succeed.

Chapter 6

The Rebirth of Joy

Weeks passed, and Adrian found himself testing Harrow's advice again and again. Each time, the pull of old habits returned—the temptation to savor another's stumble—but each time, he tried something different.

At first, it felt forced. When colleagues succeeded, his congratulations sounded hollow in his own ears, like lines read from a script. But slowly, something shifted.

One Friday afternoon, Clara called again. This time, her voice was lighter. "Remember that contract I lost? The same company came back to me for a smaller project. It's not everything, but it's a start."

Adrian braced for the familiar sting of comparison, but instead, warmth bloomed in his chest. Genuine warmth. He was happy for her—not because she had stumbled, but because she had risen again.

Later that evening, he walked through the city streets, watching strangers go about their lives. A young man held open a door for an elderly woman. A child laughed as she raced to keep up with her father.

A group of students celebrated outside a café, cheering over exam results.

Adrian realized he was smiling—not at misfortune, but at joy itself. He felt lighter than he had in years, as though some invisible weight had loosened its grip.

For so long, he had feasted on scraps of failure, mistaking them for sustenance. Now he understood: true nourishment came from a different source. Not from shadows, but from light.

He thought of Harrow's words again. "When you can find joy in others rising, you'll finally learn how to rise yourself."

And for the first time, Adrian believed them.

Reflection: Moving From Shadow to Light

This final chapter of Adrian's story marks his rebirth—the moment he discovers the deeper, more lasting joy of celebrating others' growth.

The transformation is not about denying the darker feelings we sometimes have. It's about choosing not to be ruled by them. By shifting focus from envy and misfortune to empathy and shared success, we move from *epicaricacy* to something brighter: goodwill, compassion, and mutual flourishing.

Ask Yourself:

- What would my life look like if I celebrated others' wins as much as my own?
- How would my relationships change? My confidence? My happiness?
- Am I ready to choose light over shadow?

Exercise – Practicing Eunoia

The Greek word **eunoia** means beautiful thinking or goodwill. To practice it:

1. Each day for the next month, write down one success you witnessed in someone else.
2. Note how it made you feel when you chose to celebrate it rather than envy it.
3. At the end of the month, reflect: how has your outlook shifted?

Chapter 7

Understanding Epicaricacy

Most people have felt it, even if they've never named it: the small flicker of satisfaction when a rival stumbles, when a boastful friend is humbled, when someone "too perfect" finally cracks.

That flicker has a name: **epicaricacy**.

The word itself isn't one you'll hear often in English, but its roots tell the story. In Greek, **epi** means "upon," **charis** means "joy," and **kakos** means "misfortune." Put together, they point to a strange kind of happiness—joy built on someone else's struggle. The Germans captured the same feeling with a word that's far more familiar: *Schadenfreude.* Different languages, same shadow-joy hiding in the human heart.

Why Does It Exist?

Why do we feel this way at all? Three forces tend to stir it up:

- **Comparison.** We measure ourselves against others almost without thinking. For a moment, their stumble feels like our step up.
- **Insecurity.** When we're unsure of our own worth, someone else's mistake can feel like proof that we're not failing alone.
- **A skewed sense of fairness.** If we believe someone didn't deserve their position, their fall can feel like justice served.

Shadow-joy doesn't make us evil—it makes us human. But by noticing these roots, we get the chance to pull them out before they grow deeper.

The Problem With Shadow Joy

While epicaricacy is natural, it's also hollow. The satisfaction fades quickly, often replaced by guilt, emptiness, or shame. Over time, it can:

- Weaken relationships (trust erodes when we root against people we care about).
- Stunt growth (we focus more on others' failures than on building our own success).

- Feed negativity (our happiness depends on misfortune rather than fulfillment).

This is why Adrian's story resonates: at first, the feeling gave him a rush. But eventually, it left him hungry, disconnected, and ashamed.

The good news? By bringing this shadow into the light, we gain the power to transform it.

Ask Yourself

- When was the last time you felt a flicker of satisfaction at someone else's failure?
- Did it give you lasting joy, or did it fade quickly?
- What might that moment reveal about your own comparisons, insecurities, or sense of fairness?

Exercise – Awareness Without Judgment

For the next seven days:

1. Carry a small notebook (or use a notes app on your phone).

2. Each time you notice yourself feeling epicaricacy, jot it down. Don't judge—just observe.

3. At the end of the day, review your notes. Ask: What insecurity, comparison, or justice-bias fueled this feeling?

The goal isn't to eliminate the feeling overnight. It's to **name it**, to shine a light on it. Only what is acknowledged can be transformed.

Key Insight:

Epicaricacy is not who you are—it's a reflex. And like any reflex, with awareness and practice, it can be reshaped.

Chapter 8

The True Cost of Shadow Joy

On the surface, shadow-joy may look like a small, harmless reaction. We might grin when a competitor makes a mistake, when a coworker who usually shows off falters during a meeting, or when a public figure is caught in an awkward moment. These tiny flashes of amusement often pass quickly, but repeated often enough, they leave an imprint on how we view others —and ourselves.

The costs of indulging in shadow-joy add up over time:

- **Relationships strain:** Even if no one else notices, we feel the dissonance inside when we quietly root against those around us. Trust erodes, both given and received.
- **Personal growth stalls:** Measuring ourselves by others' setbacks tricks us into believing we've advanced, when in reality we've only stood still.
- **Negativity spreads:** The more often we look for failures to savor, the more our mindset

narrows, leaving us dependent on others' losses instead of building our own wins.

Ask Yourself

- Who in my life have I unconsciously rooted against?
- How might this have affected my relationship with them?
- Do I spend more time noticing others' failures than working toward my own progress?

Exercise – Relationship Mapping

1. Write down the names of 5 people you interact with regularly (coworkers, friends, family).
2. For each, answer honestly: Do I celebrate their wins, feel indifferent, or secretly hope for their stumbles?
3. Mark the ones where shadow joy has shown up.
4. Choose one person from that list and commit this week to intentionally encouraging them—

send a kind message, congratulate them, or offer help.

This simple act begins reversing the quiet damage of epicaricacy. Where shadow joy divides, light-joy restores connection.

Key Insight:

Epicaricacy robs us twice: once by feeding us false joy, and again by stealing the real joy we could have found in growth and connection.

Chapter 9

Transforming Envy Into Inspiration

Envy and epicaricacy often walk hand in hand. Both creep in when we compare ourselves to someone else and feel a little smaller for it. Epicaricacy whispers, "Let them stumble." Envy says, "I wish they hadn't risen." But envy can also act as a guidepost. It doesn't just show us what bothers us—it reveals what we secretly value, what we hunger for in our own lives. Instead of treating envy as poison, we can treat it as a compass. When used wisely, envy can be transformed into inspiration.

1. Spot the Signal

When you envy someone, ask yourself: *What about their success stirs me?*

- Is it their discipline?
- Their courage?
- Their creativity?
- Their recognition?

Envy shows us where our own ambitions live.

2. Flip the Script

Instead of wishing the person would fail, ask: *What can I learn from them?*

- If they achieved what I want, what steps did they take?
- What habits or mindsets do they embody that I can practice too?

This doesn't mean copying them. It means letting their example ignite action in you.

3. Use Envy as Fuel

Every time you feel that pang of envy, use it as a trigger: *This is my cue to grow.* Instead of stewing in resentment, take one concrete step toward your own goal—write the draft, practice the skill, send the application.

Adrian's Shift (Story Tie-In)

When Adrian watched Maya succeed after his encouragement, he felt the tug of comparison. Part of him envied her confidence, her ease with the client. But instead of wishing her stumble, he asked himself: *What could I learn from her courage?*

That shift—from bitterness to curiosity—was where his own growth began.

Ask Yourself

- Who am I most envious of right now?
- What does their success reveal about what I secretly want for myself?
- Am I using that signal to grow, or to resent?

Exercise – Flip the Script

1. Identify one person you envy. Write their name at the top of a page.
2. List the qualities, habits, or achievements they have that spark your envy.

3. For each, reframe it: What lesson or inspiration can I take from this?

4. Commit to one small action this week that moves you closer to that quality in your own life.

Example:

- Envy: “She’s always confident in meetings.”
- Inspiration: “She prepares thoroughly and speaks with clarity.”
- Action: “I’ll rehearse my points before the next team call.”

Key Insight:

Envy doesn’t have to shrink you. When transformed, it can be a compass pointing directly toward your potential.

Chapter 10

Escaping the Comparison Trap

Comparison is wired into us. For most of human history, survival meant measuring ourselves against the tribe: *Am I strong enough to keep up? Am I skilled enough to contribute?* Comparison kept us safe.

But in today's world, constant comparison—at work, online, even within our families—has become a trap. It fuels envy, resentment, and epicaricacy. And it keeps us from the only comparison that matters: *who we were yesterday versus who we are today.*

1. Why Comparison Fails

The trouble with comparison is that it never plays fair.

- **It keeps moving the goalposts:** No matter how much we achieve, there will always be someone with more—more talent, more wealth, more recognition.
- **It tricks our eyes:** Social media, especially, shows the highlight reel while hiding the rough drafts and failures. We end up comparing our

struggles with someone else's edited version of success.

- **It blurs our direction:** The more we fixate on other people's paths, the easier it is to forget what we actually want. Before long, we're chasing their goals instead of our own.

The only real way out of this trap is to turn the lens inward: to measure today's self against yesterday's, instead of against everyone else's filtered victories.

2. The Cost of the Trap

Comparison doesn't just hurt self-esteem—it paralyzes growth. If you're always measuring against someone else, you may never take bold steps. Why try, if you'll never be "as good as them"?

3. Shifting the Lens: The Self-Comparison Principle

The only fair, useful comparison is with yourself. Who were you last month? Last year? What habits, skills, or mindsets have grown since then?

This shift doesn't erase competition. It redefines it. You are your rival. You are also your ally.

Adrian's Shift (Story Tie-In)

Adrian realized his career had been built not on his growth, but on Marcus's failures. When he began comparing himself to his *past self*—to the Adrian who once shrank in every meeting—he finally saw real progress. He wasn't trying to be Marcus anymore. He was trying to be a stronger version of himself.

Ask Yourself

- Who do I most often compare myself to, and why?
- What goals or standards am I chasing only because someone else has them?
- If I measured progress only against my past self, what growth would I see?

Exercise – The Personal Progress Journal

1. Get a notebook or digital document. Title it *My Progress Journal*.
2. At the end of each week, write:
    - One thing I did better than last week.
    - One area I still want to improve.
    - One small step I'll take next week.
3. After three months, look back. Compare yourself—not to others, but to the "you" who began this practice.

Key Insight:

Comparison to others keeps you trapped in envy and epicaricacy. Comparison to your past self frees you to grow.

Chapter 11

Choosing Shared Success

It's easy to believe success works like a limited resource—if someone else takes a bigger slice, there must be less left for us. That scarcity mindset feeds shadow-joy, because their loss feels like space opening up for us. But the truth is different. Success spreads more like fire: when one torch lights another, the flame doesn't weaken—it grows brighter. When we learn to celebrate and amplify the wins around us, we discover that their rise can actually lift us too.

1. The Scarcity Lie

Scarcity whispers: *If they win, I lose.*

This mindset keeps us guarded, competitive, and small. It limits collaboration and poisons relationships.

2. The Multiplying Truth

The truth is, most forms of success are not zero-sum. When your colleague succeeds, your team looks stronger. When your friend thrives, your circle grows richer. When your partner shines, your relationship deepens.

Joy, like knowledge and love, multiplies when shared.

3. Reframing Success as Collective

Imagine measuring success not by individual trophies, but by how much growth you foster in those around you. The paradox is this: the more you help others succeed, the more opportunities and trust come back to you.

Adrian's Shift (Story Tie-In)

When Adrian helped Maya succeed in her presentation, something surprising happened. Her win didn't diminish him—it elevated him. Clients began to see him as a leader who could bring out the best in others. His reputation grew, not by hoarding success, but by multiplying it.

Ask Yourself

- Do I secretly see success as scarce—believing others' wins take something from me?
- Who in my life could I lift up right now, without losing anything myself?

- How might my own growth accelerate if I celebrated and amplified others?

Exercise – Daily Celebration Practice

For the next 7 days:

1. Each day, choose one person in your circle.
2. Acknowledge a recent win of theirs—big or small. Congratulate them, post a supportive comment, or simply express genuine appreciation.
3. Notice how your mindset shifts when success is something to be shared, not hoarded.

Key Insight:

Success is not diminished by being shared. In fact, shared success multiplies, deepens trust, and fuels long-term growth—for you and those around you.

Chapter 12

From Epicaricacy to Eunoia

For so long, Adrian believed joy was scarce—that his satisfaction had to come from others' stumbles. But the more he lived, the more he discovered a greater truth: real joy is abundant, and the deepest form of it comes not from shadow, but from light.

Where epicaricacy once guided his reactions, a new word began to shape his life: **eunoia**.

There's a Greek word that points us toward the opposite of shadow-joy: **eunoia**. It combines *eu* ("good") and *nous* ("mind"), often translated as "beautiful thinking." But it's more than a definition—it's a way of being. Eunoia is the habit of goodwill, the choice to orient our thoughts toward harmony. If epicaricacy delights in another's stumble, eunoia finds joy in their ascent. Practicing it means expanding the number of victories we get to celebrate—because every success around us becomes, in some small way, our own.

1. The Power of Eunoia

Eunoia does more than make us "nicer people." It transforms how we live:

- **It heals relationships** by turning envy into encouragement.
- **It fuels growth** by shifting our focus to collaboration instead of rivalry.
- **It deepens joy** because celebrating others expands the sources of happiness in our lives.

When we practice eunoia, every win around us becomes another spark of joy within us. Life multiplies instead of diminishes.

2. The Practice of Eunoia

Like any habit, goodwill can be cultivated. A few daily practices can shift your mindset:

- **Celebrate Out Loud** – Don't just feel happy for others; express it. Let people know you see them and value their wins.
- **Turn Comparison Into Curiosity** – Instead of "Why not me?" ask "What can I learn from them?"

- **Anchor in Gratitude** – Each morning, list not only what you're grateful for in your own life, but also something you're grateful for in others' lives.

Adrian's Final Step (Story Tie-In)

In his last conversation with Marcus, Adrian didn't feel the old twinge of rivalry. Instead, he felt pride—pride that Marcus had pushed him, challenged him, and unknowingly guided him toward growth. For the first time, he didn't need Marcus to stumble. He could stand tall on his own—and still wish Marcus well.

That was his true rebirth: from epicaricacy to eunoia.

Ask Yourself

- How often do I feel joy at another's success?
- How could my life expand if every win in my circle became a win for me too?
- What would it look like to live with "beautiful thinking" every day?

Exercise – The Eunoia Journal

1. Each night, write down one success you witnessed in someone else.

2. Reflect on how their growth enriches your world, directly or indirectly.

3. End by writing one sentence of goodwill for them (e.g., *"May their courage keep growing"*).

Over time, you'll find your reflex shifting. Instead of shadow joy, you'll instinctively lean toward light joy.

Final Insight:

Epicaricacy is a shadow we all carry. But by recognizing it, transforming envy into inspiration, escaping comparison, and choosing shared success, we can step into something far brighter: a life of eunoia—where joy multiplies, relationships deepen, and growth becomes boundless.

Epilogue

The Beauty of Light

Adrian stood at the edge of the same city park where, years earlier, he had once watched Marcus stumble with a secret flicker of satisfaction. The trees were the same, the hum of traffic still a steady backdrop—but Adrian was no longer the same man.

He thought about the winding path that had brought him here: the envy, the hollow victories, the guilt, the mirror-breaking moments. For a long time, he had believed joy could only come from someone else's shadow. But life had taught him otherwise.

When Clara forgave him, when Maya flourished under his encouragement, when Marcus finally shook his hand without rivalry—each of those moments revealed a deeper truth. Joy was never scarce. It was never something to hoard, or steal, or secretly savor at another's expense. Joy was abundant, multiplying the more it was shared.

Adrian smiled as he watched a young boy chase his kite across the grass. The boy tripped, fell, and then laughed as his father scooped him up, cheering him on. Years ago, Adrian might have smirked at the stumble. Now, all he felt was warmth for the boy's courage and gratitude for the father's joy.

That was the difference. The shadow had lifted. The light had arrived.

He whispered the word he had once looked up in an old book, the word that had finally reshaped his heart:

Eunoia.

Beautiful thinking. Goodwill toward others. A way of living that turned every success into a shared flame.

Adrian walked on, not as a man who needed others to fail, but as a man free enough to celebrate every rise, every triumph, every piece of beauty the world had to offer.

And in that freedom, he found a joy deeper than he had ever known.

Closing Note to the Reader

Adrian's journey is not just his own—it mirrors ours. We all wrestle with epicaricacy, envy, and comparison. But we also all have the power to choose eunoia: to cultivate beautiful thinking, to celebrate shared success, and to step into a joy that multiplies without end.

The shadow will always whisper. But the light is always stronger. And the beauty of light is this: it shines brighter when shared.

Conclusion

Living with Eunoia

Every book has an ending, but transformation is a beginning. You've walked through shadows, reflected in mirrors, and learned that joy is never scarce. Now, it's time to live these lessons in daily life.

Here are three commitments you can carry forward:

1. **Choose Awareness** – Notice when envy or shadow joy stirs within you. Awareness is the first step to change.

2. **Flip to Inspiration** – Every time you feel envy, ask: *What can I learn from this?*

3. **Celebrate Shared Success** – Make it a practice to voice encouragement. The more joy you create for others, the more joy you'll feel yourself.

Transformation doesn't happen in one moment. It happens in daily choices—small, steady acts of eunoia.

As you close this book, remember: light is always stronger than shadow. And joy, when shared, is limitless.

Printed at Repro India Ltd.